Building Home-school Connection with Cell Phones

The Innovative Educator Series

Fix the School, Not the Child: 20 Ideas for Parents Who Want to Advocate for the Rights of their Child in School
ISBN 978-1-63233-018-5 ($7.99)

Building a Strong Home-School Connection with Cell Phones (with Willyn Webb)
ISBN 978-1-63233-005-5 ($7.99)

How to Opt Out (Not Drop Out) of School: A Guide for Teens for Self-Directed Education
ISBN 978-1-63233-048-2 ($7.99)

Supporting Student Personal Learning Networks
ISBN 978-1-63233-085-7 ($7.99)

The Uncomfortable History of American Schooling: 1500s -Today
ISBN 978-1-63233-091-8 ($7.99)

The Social Classroom: Engaging Learners with Cell Phones & Social Media
ISBN 978-1-63233-089-5 ($7.99)

The Working Home Educator's Guide to Success: Stories and Advice for Working Families That Want to Home Educate
ISBN 978-1-63233-087-1 ($7.99)

Building a Strong Home-School Connection with Cell Phones

by Lisa Nielsen
and Willyn Webb

an imprint of Eifrig Publishing
Lemont   Berlin

Published by Eifrig Publishing,
PO Box 66, Lemont, PA 16851.
Knobelsdorffstr. 44, 14059 Berlin, Germany

For information regarding permission, write to:
Rights and Permissions Department,
Berry Street Books, an imprint of Eifrig Publishing,
PO Box 66, Lemont, PA 16851, USA.
permissions@eifrigpublishing.com, 888-340-6543.

Library of Congress Cataloging-in-Publication Data

Nielsen, Lisa, and Willyn Webb
  Building a Strong Home-School Connection
with Cell Phones

 / by Lisa Nielsen and Willyn Webb.
     p.   cm.

Paperback: ISBN 978-1-63233-005-5
Ebook: ISBN 978-1-63233-069-7

     1. Education 2. Reform 3. Media
     I. Nielsen, Lisa, and Willyn Webb II. Title.

25 24 23 22 2021
5 4 3 2

Printed on acid-free paper. ∞

TABLE OF CONTENTS

INTRODUCTION

As a teacher, principal, counselor, parent coordinator or any school staff that works with students, you know the importance of the home-school connection. However, many still don't realize the power of the tool that many teens, and even some adults, describe as another appendage - the cell phone. Even if they don't have Internet access, most of our students' families have access to cell phones or mobile devices.

Many families who don't even have a landline, now have a cell phone. According to the "Cell Phone Nation" Marist Poll (2009) 94% of households have access to a cell phone. For many, the cell phone is not only the best, but the primary way to reach parents. "As of December

2011, 34 percent of American households were wireless-only" (Blumberg & Luke, 2011). These facts prove crucial in demonstrating cell phones as a key tool we have right now to bridge the digital divide and strengthen the home-school connection. Simply use a phone as a calling and texting device? It's time we changed!

Through cell phones, students and individuals can connect with many free and easy-to- use resources that can help schools communicate, coordinate and connect with parents in powerful and exciting ways. In fact, we can learn a lot from the business world regarding the value of cell phones in making connections. In addition, marketing experts have compiled a host of relevant statistics and, as a result, turned their attention to the tool that will get their message directly to consumers - cell phones. Educators should do the same. Our interactions with parents and students will benefit, as explained through the tools presented in this book. If we want to reach parents in a timely and convenient way, the cell phone is obviously the way to go.

Let's take a look at some of those statistics:

It takes 90 minutes for the average person to respond to an email. It takes 90 seconds for the average person to respond to a text message.

91% of all U.S. citizens have their mobile device within reach 24/7.

It takes 26 hours for the average person to report a lost wallet. It takes 68 minutes for them to report a lost phone.

There are 6.8 billion people on the planet. 5.1 billion of them own a cell phone, but only 4.2 billion own a toothbrush.

There are more mobile phones on the planet than there are TVs.

Despite the prevalence of cell phones, "88% of schools still ban classroom use for learning," according to a recent study (Tru, 2012). For educators interested in changing this statistic, start with parents. When adults see the value of cell phone tools, they will be more likely to support classroom use of these devices. Adults already place heavy value on their cell phones. In fact, "For some, the anxious feeling that they might miss something has caused them to slumber next to their smartphones." In fact, according to the Pew Research Center, two-thirds of adults sleep with their phones right next to their beds (Gibson, 2011). The cell phone has quickly become the most ubiquitous tool in households today. Educators should not ignore this treasured device as a useful tool in building supportive relationships with parents and thus benefiting their students' education. Everybody wins for a change.

As a premise, building these home-school relationships become invaluable. As stated in the Harvard Family Research Project, "Good communication between parents and teachers has many benefits. Most importantly, children benefit by improved communication because contact between home and school helps children learn and succeed. But parent-teacher communication can also be hard, especially when parents feel uncomfortable in school, don't speak English well, or come from different cultural backgrounds than teachers" (Kreider, Mayer, & Vaughan, 1999). When parents don't feel comfortable in their child's school or with verbal communication due to language or cultural barriers, texting is the perfect way to empower them and enable the communication. Through texting, parents are able to read and translate teachers' texts and then form a reply and send it, most likely with the help of a friend, family member, or even their child. Programs and easy-to-use apps exist to translate all languages, making it a step easier. In short, more parents can communicate with more teachers about their kids.

While the use of these digital tools may seem foreign territory to many educators and administrators, in their book Teaching Generation Text: Using Cell Phones to Enhance Learning, Lisa Nielsen and Willyn Webb provide a plan for harnessing the power of cell phones for learning. They explain that strengthening the home-school connection with cell phones can be an important step in the ultimate learning process.

TEXTING & VOICE

Now let's look at how texting and voice can develop and strengthen relationships between home and school and also learn how the following tools can provide a foundation to understanding and realizing the benefits of cell phone use to learning:

TEXTING
Remind 101 (www.remind101.com)
Twitter (www.Twitter.com)
Mobile Commons (www.mobilecommons.com)
Cel.ly (www.cel.ly.com)
PollEverywhere (www.polleverywhere.com)
Classpager (www.classpager.com)
LocaModa (wiffiti.locamoda.com)

VOICE
Robocalls
Personal Phone Calls
Free Conference Call (www.freeconferencecall.com)
iPadio (www.ipadio.com)
Voki (www.voki.com)
Google Voice (www.google.com/voice)

I. TEXTING

Texting, in many ways, has made communication easier. According to the Pew Research Center, 72% of teenagers text regularly, and one in three sends more than 100 texts per day Lenhart, Ling, Campbell, & Purcell, (2010). Clearly texting is a preferred method of communication among young people and that trend is moving upward toward adults, who also text much more frequently in recent years.

According to the National School Public Relations Association (2011), receiving information through electronic communication is among the top choices of parents and families for receiving information. This is especially useful when trying to connect with hard to reach parents. Parents who are on the go, busy, or prefer multitasking will generally appreciate a teacher who texts. The following tools provide some great ways to digitally reach out to parents and families:

Remind 101 (https://www.remind101.com)

Remind101 is a safe, one-way, mass text messaging system created specifically for use in education. It keeps your phone number, and the phone numbers of your subscribers completely private, stores all of your sent messages and it's completely free to use. Once the school's parent coordinator signs up and creates a parent list, parents are able to sign up with one text or email.

Districts like Clarkstown Central School District in New York have found the tool extremely useful for quick, in-the-moment, updates. After hurricane Sandy this past fall one district administrator wrote, "In fewer than 48 hours, more than 2,000 community members benefited from Remind101 service by receiving text messages related to the state of our schools. While I've known Remind101 to be a fantastic communication tool for teachers and students, I never dreamed it would be such a lifesaver for us in our time of need."

Because of the convenience of sending messages directly to parents' phones, Remind101 is a perfect tool for announcements and reminders such as school holidays, school events, photo days, fundraising events, testing days and more.

Twitter (www.Twitter.com)

Anyone (in the US) can receive Tweets on their phone even if they haven't signed up for Twitter. This is a simple way for people to get information they care about in real-time. For example, let's say you want to get Tweets from New York City Schools (@NYCSchools). Just text 'follow NYCSchools' to 40404.

Suggesting parents follow their district's Twitter account can serve as a powerful way to keep parents informed of up to date information. For example, during the 2013 Nor'easter in New York, the @NYCSchools Twitter account provided up-to-date information on school closing and after school activities in both English and Spanish:

NYC Public Schools @NYCSchools

Schools are open today, but afterschool programs and PSAL games are cancelled. Please visit nyc.gov for the latest info.

Gobierno de NYC □@nycgob

Alcade: Las actividades despuйs de clases y juegos PSAL estбn canceladas. Actividades y clases @NYCSchools el sбbado estarбn canceladas.

It doesn't have to stop with following your school district. Schools, principals and even teachers can set up Twitter accounts to keep parents connected to the latest information. Check out how this worked at Locke Elementary School in this video: youtu.be/GyQz48V6UmM

Mobile Commons (www.mobilecommons.com)

Is today a school holiday or snow day?

When are parent-teacher conferences? When is the deadline to register for high school entrance exams? If your district offers a texting service, this is the type of information you can find in a snap.

Places like New York City are using a texting service called <u>Mobile Commons</u> to keep public school families informed with text messages in English or Spanish throughout the school year by texting "nycschools" or "escuela" to 877877. New York City's Mayor Michael Bloomberg touted the program as a crucial step in "doing more to make sure parents have the information they need to help their children succeed – even when they are on the go."

Cel.ly (www.cel.ly.com)

Cel.ly is a free, mobile social network that works via group texting. It is instant, private, and secure. There is never an exchange of personal cell phone numbers, yet everyone is connected in the ways that work best depending on the need.

Each cell is its own mobile social network that works with any mobile phone or device. Members can join instantly with one text and exchange group messages, polls, reminders and web alerts. There is a record of all texts sent and received.

School guidance counselor Willyn Webb says that Cel.ly has made a positive improvement for her school's Parent Accountability Committee (PAC) which meets once per month. Before Cel.ly, she found it frustrating to provide a clear picture of school happenings during a monthly meeting. Willyn's solution: invite them all to join her PAC Cell! She did this at a meeting by sharing the Cel.ly number and Cell name. It's so easy to join. They just took out their phones and within the first five minutes of the meeting, it was in place.

At first this team just communicated about logistics. For example, Webb used Cel.ly to set up a last minute Christmas potluck for their December meeting. Today, Webb sends a daily message that might be to share progress regarding service learning projects, academic milestones, praises for students and staff, struggles, and needs for improvement. The parents remain welcome to respond, and if warranted, a powerful response might be re-sent to the group.

During the few seconds it takes to send a single text, parents truly become part of the day to day happenings at Delta Opportunity School. Parents have shared that this helps them do their job better, look more forward to meetings, and truly advocate for their school and the students.

As a result of Cel.ly the PAC is now communicating often, and Webb says she feels great about keeping her PAC up-to-date and informed with the praises, growth and challenges.

PollEverywhere (www.polleverywhere.com)

Poll Everywhere provides a terrific way to capture the thoughts, ideas and opinions of parents. Simply set up a multiple choice or free response poll, text parents the code, and have them text in their answers like they do on shows like American Idol.

Poll Everywhere provides a quick and easy way to give parents a voice and a vote. For example, ever wonder how much homework kids are getting a night, how long parents spend helping their children with schoolwork, or how many hours students are sleeping each night? Massachusetts Ed Tech Specialist, Tracy Sockalosky, suggests collecting such information by using Poll Everywhere to send out a poll to find out. Not only is this a great way to collect information, but it's also a terrific discussion starter, as well as a tool to determine areas of concern. Eric Sheninger, principal of New Milford High School in New Jersey, suggests using Poll Everywhere during back to school nights. He says it's a great way to elicit feedback during budget presentations, or to secure real-time input on school initiatives. Laura Spencer, an instructional technology coordinator for a K-8 school district in San Diego, suggests quizzing students on topics taught in school with a twist. She also sends the messages to parents. She explains that students enjoy comparing their responses to their parents, and this gives parents a deeper insight into what is happening during the school day. Maine school board member, Lisa Cooley, suggests using Poll Everywhere to seek out parent opinions or feedback on a recent school event, a new facility, the holiday homework or a new curriculum.

Classpager (https://www.classpager.com)

Connect with parents and engage students with polls, exit tickets, event reminders and more with ClassPager. ClassPager allows parents and students to use their own devices (phones, tablets, laptops, or other computers) to respond to questions or surveys that the teachers design. Questions can be both open response and multiple choice.

Amar Vedi, an Algebra and Statistics teacher at Vance High School in North Carolina, uses ClassPager to assign homework, send out reminders, share links to educational videos and answer questions. In many cases, Classpager can also be sent to parents as well as students, to keep them apprised of what is taking place in his classroom. What a relief for parents who routinely struggle with kids to drag out homework assignments. Indeed, Vedi has noticed that it's been a great tool for improving his communication with individual students and parents. He explains that because of this easy collaboration between students, parents, and himself, there has been a marked improvement in classroom culture and student achievement.

II. VOICE

If you are old enough to read this, you may be old enough to remember the days of the rotary phone and advertisements encouraging us to reach out and touch someone. Even those who aren't tech savvy still know how to make a phone call and even those who embrace technology cannot deny the personal benefit of a live voice to voice conversation. In fact, now more than ever, it shows how much you care if you are willing to utilize voice.

This used to be more time consuming. However, using cell phones along with the services that follow can provide time-saving tools, so that when the situation calls for it or the teacher wants a more personal interaction, voice remains an option. All of us, even the technology shy, have the skills necessary to take advantage of numerous free resources available to connect and coordinate with parents in innovative ways by just picking up the phone and making a call. The personal connection is definitely an enhancement.

Here are some resources to make that possible:

Robocalls

Wikipedia defines a Robocall as a term for a phone call that uses a computerized auto-dialer to deliver a pre-recorded message, as if from a robot (hence the name). Services like Dial My Calls (www.dialmycalls.com) provide this option which can be a lifeline for schools in times of emergency such as natural disasters.

Robocalling can also be used to deliver a standardized message to homes, such as snow days and follow-up when a child is tardy. Delta Opportunity School in Colorado makes robocalls home whenever a student is absent. While this is a great way to send home auto messages, many parents stop answering at the time of day of the computer call and let it go to voicemail. The robocalls becomes an effective way to deliver information, but when there is a concern, the personal touch is lost. Guidance counselor, Willyn Webb realized this issue and addressed it by using our next resource.

Personal Phone Calls

We couldn't have a section on using voice without mentioning the old-school phone call, which addresses the issue of impersonalization that can occur with the sole use robocalling. When it seems it might be helpful, possibly as a follow up to robocalls, Webb calls homes at a different time than when the computer calls. Recently, when she did this, her student's mother answered and Webb was able to shared a concern about her son being absent. When the mother jumped into excuses, Webb explained that she didn't call to get her son into trouble, but rather to express personal concern about him and to ensure he had the support needed to best adjust to the school.

This mother appeared relieved and moved about the personal outreach. This opened the door to a great discussion about how his individualized learning plan, what he liked and didn't like about the school, his health issues and more. It also allowed Webb to develop a connection with the family, resulting in a ripple effect of caring, and consequently, her son attending school regularly.

While robocalls certainly have their place, we must acknowledge the importance of a personal phone call for convincing parents that school staff truly cares.

Free Conference Call

(www.freeconferencecall.com)

Free Conference Call can be used by sharing a phone number and a conference call code to participate in a live call that can bring parents together to listen in to a lecture, meeting or simply engage in a group discussion. The website has many features, including a post call e-mail detailing the number of callers and the length of the call.

Each free teleconferencing account accommodates up to 96 callers on an unlimited number of conference calls which can last up to 6 hours. Long distance charges may apply, but nothing additional from FreeConferenceCall. com. FreeConferenceCall accounts also come with FREE conference call recording! So not only do we enjoy the recording service free, it's accessible by phone or computer with no additional charges for downloading. You can distribute, archive or even send recordings to your listeners via RSS and podcast – for FREE. To access the free teleconference recording features, just visit FreeConferenceCall.com and register for a recording account. You will receive instant account access with recording passwords and playback instructions.

iPadio (www.ipadio.com)

Wouldn't it be great to have a weekly podcast for parents? While the idea sounds good, when we think of podcasting, it often seems confusing and hard to put together. Not so with a phonecasting service like iPadio. All you need to know how to do is dial a phone number and speak. Then boom! Your phonecast is instantly published and can be shared via your website, blog, email or text.

Sixth grade language arts and social studies teacher Josh Stumpenhorst creates phonecasts for his class in Naperville, IL. He uses phonecasts as a way to communicate classroom happenings to parents and students. This window into his classroom provides students, their families and others interested school community members with up to date information about what is actually being done in class.

Teachers can use iPadio to bridge the home-school connection by wearing a basic headset that can be used with every cell phone and recording unit mini lessons with iPadio. This is a great way for absentee students to catch up with their class, for students who need a lesson review, as well as for parents who are wondering, "What did my child learn in school today?" Teachers could even record several mini lessons in advance of a unit and allow students to flow through at their own pace.

Students could help create phone casts too, to share school news, upcoming events, students of the month or celebrate student work and/or teacher successes.

Voki (www.voki.com)

Voki provides a great way to stay connected with parents. With Voki, you can share a personalized message using a customizable animated avatar along with your own voice recorded right from your phone. You can design your avatar's appearance, add voice, and get an embed code to pop it into any web2.0 compatible site (Wikis, Blogs, Facebook, Websites) or even an old school PowerPoint. The avatar moves and speaks based on what you say.

Since Vokis are easily embeddable, school

staff often use Voki to record introduction messages for their school websites. For example, special education teacher Kim Gill embedded a Voki to welcome students and parents on her homepage. (teachers.wrdsb. ca/gillk). Primary school Principal Greg Miller recorded a personalized welcome message and embedded onto the school website which you can see here. Primary school enrichment teacher Jennifer Matthews has students create Vokis to show what they know. She places their Vokis onto the class page of her website and shares them with parents to give provide insight into what their children are learning in class.

Not only does Voki provide a fun way to share information with parents, but you can also capture anyone's message with a cell phone. In other words, once you set up a Voki on any computer, you can hand a phone to a student, teacher, principal or yourself to capture powerful words or ideas to share.

Google Voice (www.google.com/voice**)**

Contact is key. Parents want school staff accessible. However, 24/7 access isn't always possible, nor should it be realistically. Chris Casal, the technology teacher & tech coordinator at PS 10 Brooklyn uses his Google Voice number on a daily basis to keep the parent-teacher lines of communication open and accessible as well as serve as a point of contact available to all members of the school community.

Google Voice (GVoice) is a free service through Google. If you are a Google Apps school or just have a Gmail account, you can get a GVoice phone number by visiting www.google.com/voice/?setup=1#setup. If you don't have a Gmail account you can create one for free at www.gmail.com.

Here's how it works. Google Voice lets you select a standard phone number to tie to your email account. You can have that GVoice number call multiple phones, or none. In addition, the calls &

voicemails can be forwarded to your Gmail inbox, an app on your smartphone or tablet, and you can reply via those methods too. GVoice takes the actual phone out of the equation and makes the concept of the phone number accessible across all modern technology platforms.

School staff will find Google Voice useful in connecting and coordinating with parents in a number of ways. For example, you can let Google Voice be your personal secretary, transcribing your messages, allowing you to skip messages from callers you don't want to hear from, and inviting you to "eavesdrop" as a message is being left for you. Another way Google Voice can be used is by recording yourself. Just leave yourself a Google voicemail to capture a recording with important information for parents. That message can later be emailed or texted to parents.

If you're looking for a way to stay connected and provide parents with a sense of unfettered access without your phone ringing off the hook,

Google Voice may be just the thing. It is a free, simple way to offer a single point of contact you can access in various ways, often replying more quickly since you are not reliant on a single voicemail box or physical handset.

CONCLUSION

Utilizing cell phones, the tool most commonly available in the homes of our students' families, can improve communication, enhance relationships and model 21st century skills, by developing a school climate that supports student success. This is not just a trend, but a developing area where we must focus in order to stay connected. The home-school connection remains as important to education as advertising is to business and according to the Interactive Advertising Bureau, "Mobile generated significant growth – almost doubling year-over-year – up 95% to $1.2 billion in half-year 2012 from $636 million in the comparable 2011 period." As educators we can more than "double" our effectiveness in connecting with parents by utilizing the tools shared above.

We know you will find some of these resources helpful in building the home-school connection where you work. When you do, please keep the conversation going by giving us a fllow on Twitter - Lisa Nielsen (@InnovativeEdu) and Willyn Webb (@WillynWebb), connecting with us on Classroom 2.0 in our Cell phones in education group www.classroom20.com/group/CellPhonesinEducation, joining our Facebook groups at www.facebook.com/groups/TeachingGenerationText and www.facebook.com/groups/TheInnovativeEducator. And please read our blog at www.InnovativeEducator.com.

REFERENCE CHART OF KEY TERMS - TEXTING

Here is a quick guide to the ideas and resources mentioned in this chapter that will help get you on the road to strengthening the home-school connection with cell phones.

Text Tool	Definition	URL
Remind 101	A safe way for teachers to send text messages to students and stay in touch with parents. Free.	www.remind101. com
Twitter	Connect with others. Share information, discover ideas, question things. Free.	www.Twitter. com
Mobile Commons	Allows clients to reach audiences via texting with a platform that provides powerful data analysis tools that track every text, click, and call, for far-ranging insights about your audience.	www. mobilecommons. com
Celly	Mobile social networks, group texting, study groups, clickers and polling, Designed for education. Free.	cel.ly

Poll Everywhere	Text-to-screen applications for SMS voting and text walls that can be displayed on the web or in Keynote/PowerPoint.	www.polleverywhere.com
Classpager	Polls, exit tickets, event reminders, feedback. Students or parents use their own devices to respond to questions or surveys designed by the teacher using text messaging. Free.	www.classpager.com

REFERENCE CHART OF KEY TERMS - VOICE

Terms / Tools	Definition	URL
Dial My Calls	Robocalling service.	www.dialmycalls.com
Free Conference Call	Free reservationless phone conferencing.	www.freeconferencecall.com
iPadio	Broadcast live to the web from a phone call.	ipadio.com
Voki	Create Avatars and give them your voice through a phone call. Share live or post on any blog, website, or profile. Free.	www.voki.com

| Google Voice | One phone number that all of your numbers can tie to. Manage voicemails more effectively by saving them online as transcribed messages. You can also set custom voicemail greetings for different callers, listen to voicemails as they are left, and record conversations. Free. | www.google.com/voice |

JB JOSSEY-BASS TEACHER   GRADES 5–12

TEACHING
GENERATION TEXT

Using **Cell Phones**
to Enhance Learning

LISA NIELSEN · WILLYN WEBB

FOREWORD BY MARC PRENSKY

References / Recommended Reading

Gibson, E. (2011, Jul 26). Sleep with your iPhone? You're not alone. *Associated Press.* Retrieved from: www.pewinternet.org/Media-Mentions/2011/Sleep-with-your-iPhone-Youre-not-alone.aspx#

Interactive Advertising Bureau, (2012, Oct, 11). *Internet ad revenues rise to historic $17 billion in first half 2012, up 14% over half-year 2011,* Retrieved from: www.iab.net/about_the_iab/recent_press_releases/press_release_archive/press_release/pr-101112

Kreider, H., Mayer, E., & Vaughan, P. (1999). Helping parents communicate better with schools. Harvard Family Research Project. Retrieved from:

www.hfrp.org/publications-resources/browse-our-publications/helping-parents-communicate-better-with-schools

Lenhart, A., Ling, R, Campbell, S. & PUrcell, K. (2010, Apr 20). Teens and mobile phones. Retrieved from: pewinternet.org/Reports/2010/Teens-and-Mobile-Phones.aspx)

Marist Poll. (2010, June 12). *Cell phone nation.* Retrieved from: maristpoll.marist.edu/612-cell-phone-nation

National School Public Relations Association (2011). *National survey pinpoints communication preferences in school*

communication. Retrieved from:
www.nspra.org/files/docs/Release%20on%20CAP%20
Survey.pdf

Nielsen, L., & Webb, W. (2011). *Teaching generation text: Using cell phones to enhance learning.* New York, NY: Jossey-Bass.

SMSMarketingNW, (2012, March 5). Mobile Stats 2012. Retrieved from:
www.smsmarketingnw.com/category/mobile-statistics/

Tru (2012) *Verizon foundation survey on middle school students' use of mobile technology.* Retrieved from:
www.thinkfinity.org/servlet/JiveServlet/
previewBody/10549-102-2-18289/Research%20on%20
Mobile%20Technology.pdf

NOTES